Whitby
in old picture postcards

by
Alan Pickup

European Library - Zaltbommel/Netherlands MCMLXXXIII

About the Author
Mr. Alan Pickup is a keen collector of old postcards and prints with particular interest in the Ryedale area of North Yorkshire. Other books in this series he has written are on Pickering, Scarborough and York in Old Picture Postcards.

Acknowledgements
I am greatly indebted to Mr. Colin Bullamore of Sleights, a member of staff of Whitby School, for the loan of many of the original cards included in this book.

GB   ISBN 90 288 2437 5

European Library in Zaltbommel/Netherlands publishes among other things the following series:

IN OLD PICTURE POSTCARDS *is a series of books which sets out to show what a particular place looked like and what life was like in Victorian and Edwardian times. A book about virtually every town in the United Kingdom is to be published in this series. By the end of this year about 75 different volumes will have appeared. 1,250 books have already been published devoted to the Netherlands with the title* **In oude ansichten.** *In Germany, Austria and Switzerland 500, 60 and 15 books have been published as* **In alten Ansichten;** *in France by the name* **En cartes postales anciennes** *and in Belgium as* **En cartes postales anciennes** *and/or* **In oude prentkaarten** *150 respectively 400 volumes have been published.*

For further particulars about published or forthcoming books, apply to your bookseller or direct to the publisher.

This edition has been printed and bound by Grafisch Bedrijf De Steigerpoort in Zaltbommel/Netherlands.

INTRODUCTION

Anyone looking at Whitby in 1890 must have come to the conclusion how well off it was for both churches of all denominations and clergymen. At St. Mary's the Parish Church Cannon Austin was rector and he had no less than seven curates to assist him with St. Hilda's West Cliff, St. John the Evangelist, Baxtergate, St. Michael's, Church Street, and St. Ninian's, Baxtergate.

The Wesleyan Methodists had first begun to worship in the town about 1750 and in 1788 built a chapel in Church Street where John Wesley preached at the opening. This building was originally approached through an alley with houses on either side, but R.E. Pannet bought the property and demolished it. The original cost of the church was £1,200. In 1814 the Wesleyans built another church in Brunswick Street which could hold 1,100 and an organ was added in 1833. In November 1889 a meeting was held to con-

sider rebuilding the chapel as numerous complaints had been made as to how unsightly the exterior was, about uncomfortable pews and defective ventilation. The aim was to replace it with a building which would hold 900 of whom 500 would be on the ground floor and the estimate for this was £5,500. The circuit was served by three ministers and there was a mission chapel off Flowergate which had been erected in 1837 by George Miller.

The Primitive Methodist Chapel in Church Street had been built in 1821 at a cost of £1,000 and twenty years later was rebuilt and enlarged so it could seat 650. Fishburn Park Primitive Methodist Church had been built in 1866 to hold 330 at a cost of £1,100.

The Unitarian Chapel at the foot of Flowergate had an interesting history. It had been built in 1715 and then rebuilt in 1812 and could seat but 100 folk. The ministers had originally belonged to the Church of

Scotland, but it was during the lengthy pastorate of fifty-six years of Reverend Thomas Watson that the theology preached there developed into Unitarianism and in 1890 the Minister was Reverend F.H. Williams. The United Presbyterian Chapel in Cliff Street was connected with the Church of Scotland and had been put up in 1790 to seat 450 and from 1806 to 1848 Reverend George Young ministered there, but in 1890 it was served by Reverend George Robertson.

Trinity Presbyterian Church of England in Flowergate had been built in 1877/88 by public subscription at a cost of £5,600 to accommodate 500 and at this time Reverend G.M. Storrar was there.

The Congregational Church, West Cliff, was opened in 1868 at a cost of £ 5,000 and could hold 950 with a spire 120 feet high. There was also a mission chapel on The Cragg and a mission sundayschool in Church Street at this time with Reverend E. Fox Thomas in charge.

St. Hilda's Catholic Church in Bagdale had Reverend Randerson as priest in charge and he had an assistant. As if this choice of places of worship was not enough there was a Friend's Meeting House in Church Street, Salvation Army Barracks, as they were called then, in Baxtergate, and a Christadelphian meeting room at St. Ann's Staith.

Whitby at this time was represented on the County Council by R.E. Pannet and Col. J.M. Clayhills, who four years earlier, in 1886, had contested the Parliamentary seat as Gladstonian candidate only to be defeated by Ernest W. Beckett Conservative by a majority of 1,138 votes.

The Post Office in Baxtergate was open from 7 a.m. until 8 p.m. and Saturdays 9 a.m. to 8 p.m. and on Sundays from 8 to 10 a.m. and again from 5 to 6 p.m.

1. Whitby East Cliff, showing the many cottages clustering on the hillside with un made up paths and the lines of washing hung across the yards.

RELIABLE SERIES. R1738

2. Argument's Yard about 1912, which is but one of the many quaint passages and alleyways which gives the town so much of its character.

3. This card of 1906 shows a character complete with bowler hat trying to lead a donkey up the steep slope by the side of 199 steps leading up to the Abbey.

WHITBY ABBEY. – THE WESTERN GATEWAY
BEFORE & AFTER
THE GERMAN BOMBARDMENT. DEC: 16TH. 1914.

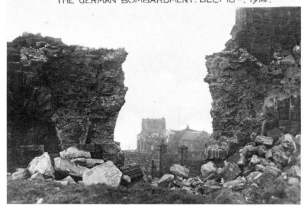

4. After the German bombardment of Scarborough on 16 December 1914 the ships sailed north and proceeded to shell Whitby. This card shows the western gateway to the Abbey before and after the German bombardment.

East Cliff, Whitby

5. Looking over to the East Cliff with an old paddle steamer crowded with visitors and crowds lining the harbour side pre-1903. Rowing boats packed with people are following and a crowd is gathered on the jetty.

WHITBY HARBOUR

6. This harbour side scene goes back to pre-1905. On the left is the Buck Hotel and next to it a cycle shop. The white border on the front of the card indicates that the space had to be used for a message if the card was going abroad as the back could still only be used for this purpose for inland correspondance.

23176. WHITBY DONKEYS. — JUDGES' LTD.

7. Donkey rides for children have long been a feature of the British sea side scene and these three Whitby donkeys are patiently waiting for young customers.

8. This superb picture showing the ruins of the West Nave of Whitby Abbey is by a local photographer called Ross and is pre-1918.

Railway Bridge after the flood Sleights

9. This is the railway bridge at Ruswarp, Whitby, littered with debry, including a rowing boat on the railway track after the disasterous floods of July 23rd, 1930.

Damaged by floods n' Glaisdale.
23-7-30,

10. This very spectacular shot shows the railway bridge at Glaisdale, Whitby, which was completely demolished by the flood waters on July 23rd, 1930. The railway track remains intact suspended in mid air looking more like a telegraph wire than a railway line.

1. Watson, Lythe.

11. This quaint circular thatched building, which appears to have a chimney, was known as The Hermitage and was to be found in Mulgrave Woods, Whitby, and is certainly pre-1918.

12. This wonderful character study is of John The Whitby Town Crier. His poster is advertising a furniture sale on October 25th, 1904. In the background is a chemist's shop. Note his bell to draw attention to his announcements and the fact that his right leg is considerably shorter than his left one.

13. This is the scene of the fatal accident on Blue Bank, Sleights near Whitby, when a char-a-banc failed to negotiate the steep hill on July 22nd, 1929 and crashed into the cottage on the hillside. Four passengers were killed and a further eight were seriously hurt. A number of other shots of this tragedy are known to exist and I am anxious to locate them.

14. This covered waggon pulled by two horses, seen at the corner of Flowergate, Whitby, must go back to the turn of the century.

Hospital Ship "Rohilla" Wrecked near Whitby Oct 30-14. Rel.

15. This shows the remains of the hospital ship Rohilla, registered at Glasgow, which sank off Whitby during the First World War on 30 October 1914 with the loss of several lives.

HOSPITAL STEAMER "ROHILLA," OF GLASGOW,
WRECKED AT WHITBY, OCTOBER 30TH, 1914
FUNERAL OF VICTIMS.

16. The coffins of the victims of the wrecked hospital ship Rohilla, which sank off Whitby on October 30th, 1914, being laid to rest. Each coffin was carried on a flat cart pulled by a horse and was escorted by Boy Scouts on the journey round the harbour side. Huge crowds turned out to pay their last respects.

Ruswarp, Whitby.

RELIABLE SERIES. 948/4

17. The only sign of life at all on this card of 1913 is a horse and cart and one other horse by the railway crossing gates at Ruswarp, Whitby. This gives a very clear view of the old road bridge over the river Esk.

Whitby Abbey.

18. This card of 1916 records what is one of the most well-known and traditional cards of Whitby. The abbey ruins with cattle grazing peacefully in the background.

Whitby—West Cliff Saloon and West Cliff.

19. This card showing the West Cliff and the West Cliff Saloon was sent to convey Christmas Greetings for Christmas 1904. It seems strange to us today that a view card of this type should have been used for this purpose, but at that time it was quite common place to do this.

RUNSWICK

20. This shows the cottages nestling at the foot of the steep cliffs at Runswick Bay, Whitby. It is on the way to Whitby from the north by the coast route. This is from a painting by the artist A.R. Quinton.

The Way to Church (199 Steps), Whitby

21. This card of 1913 shows visitors making the long and steep climb up the famous 199 steps to the church. It was obviously a very hot day as a parasol is in evidence and it must have been a very tiring climb for these ladies in their long dresses complete with long sleeves.

22. This view of Whitby Harbour, taken from the Town Station, with the Angel Hotel Vaults clearly shown certainly did impress the sender in 1919 who wrote: *We are delighted with the country and sea, together with the high cliffs and mountainous scenery makes the surroundings both beautiful and bracing.*

Whitby from Larpool.

RELIABLE SERIES. 01906

23. This view of Whitby from Larpool in 1904 failed to impress the writer who remarked:
It is not nearly so nice as it appears to be. Not a patch on Scarborough.

24. This harbour scene is pre-1906. Clustered in the centre foreground are three places of worship which reflects the strong traditions of seafarers and religion.

25. Although there were many tragedies off the North East Coast, this picture is a happier nautical scene as it shows the paddle steamer Bilsdale crowded with holiday makers. This photo was taken at Whitby with the Abbey and the church in the background.

26. It was on the 28th of December 1930 that the Swedish vessel Lucy came aground near Kettleness. Then some fifteen months later the fate of this luckless Swedish steamer was finally settled when on March 22nd, 1931 the Lucy was burnt out at Sandsend, Whitby.

Ugthorpe Mill

27. This well-known landmark is the windmill at Ugthorpe near Whitby. Sadly like so many other windmills it is no longer working today although it was in 1930. It is a pity that in those days there were no preservation orders to protect such buildings.

28. The harbour mouth at Whitby showing the lighthouse, which is a landmark for all the cargo vessels making for port.

29. A beach scene and these entertainers have certainly gathered a good crowd to watch their performance. The bathing hut on the right has an advert painted on the side which reads: 'A live paper for women Mrs. Bull, Tuesdays 1d.' On the left are three more bathing huts actually in the water, but there is not a naked body in sight!

WEST DOOR, WHITBY ABBEY.

30. The west door of Whitby Abbey makes a most impressive 'picture frame' for the view beyond.

31. The Ghaut, one of many of these very narrow little streets which provides the visitor with a surprise view of the harbour. Originally all these old properties would have been occupied by old fisher families.

32. Caedmon's Cross looking over the harbour to the hotels on the West Cliff. Today many of these are now converted into self catering holiday flats to meet the style of today's holiday makers.

33. The disaster that took place about the turn of the century at Beggar's Bridge, Glaisdale. This covered waggon was being pulled by two horses; something frightened the first horse and it jumped over the bridge taking the second horse with it. This dramatic picture shows the second horse still hanging, strangled by its own harness. The first horse has been cut down and is dead in the stream below.

34. Just putting the finishing touches to Whitby school 1912. The workmen are rolling the tarmac paths by hand. The narrow guage railway line in the foreground was used to carry bricks. The school has only had three headmasters in all these years.

35. These six horses pulling this wood cant are at Sneaton near Whitby. The date 1908 and the landlord of the pub is Thomas Lowther.

SEA WRECKED HOUSE. STAITHES. A. O. BRUCE

36. This house at Staithes near Whitby was wrecked by the sea before 1905. The chap on the right with the pair of wheels is helping remove belongings.

37. These brave women of Runswick Bay near Whitby launched the lifeboat to save their husbands on April 12th, 1901. Even to this day some of the women who live at Staithes still wear these bonnets and aprons.

GLEN ESK
NEAR WHITBY

38. These three Edwardian ladies are taking a stroll and pausing to admire the view at Glen Esk near Whitby pre-1905.

Awaiting the return of the Boats, near Staithes.

39. These fisherfolk are awaiting the return of the boats near Staithes so that they can set about unloading and preparing the catch for market.

40. The message on the back reads a young man who is in business for himself. He would go round the streets selling milk from the cans carried by the donkey. The period: during the First World War.

FRANK GOMEZ AND THE MUNICIPAL ORCHESTRA, WHITBY 1924

41. Frank Gomez and the Municipal Orchestra which played at Whitby in 1924. Note the one lady.

WHITBY REGATTA. *FINISH OF LIFEBOAT RACE.*

42. No history of Whitby would be complete without mention of the annual regatta. This card showing the finish of the lifeboat race goes back to about 1910. Yet the regatta is just as popular today seventy-five years on!

Ruswarp Mill
Burnt Down Sept 25th 1911

43. Ruswarp Mill, which was gutted by fire on September 25th, 1911. It is an odd coincidence that that was also the year that Amotherby Mill near Malton was burnt down. The comments on the reverse was that when they went to see it the following morning it was still burning.

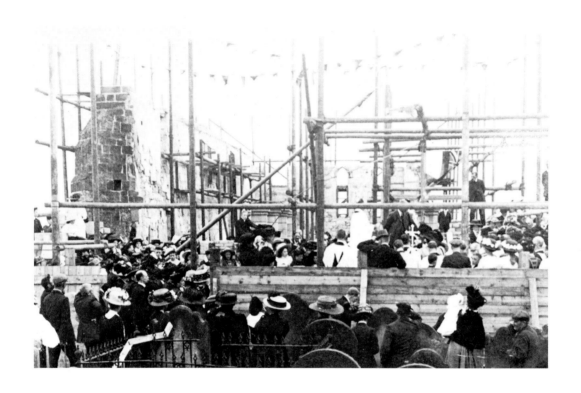

44. The foundation stone laying ceremony of St. Oswald's Church Lyth, September 29th, 1910.

45. The crowds streaming out of St. Mary's Church in their Sunday best. It must have been extremely hot as most of them have parasols up and the young men are in straw boaters.

46. The planting of the penny hedge in 1906. This was an annual event and the test was to see if it could withstand so many tides...

47. The opening of the new Primitive Methodist Church at Ruswarp near Whitby, August 17th, 1910. The church is decorated with bunting and all the ladies are out in their finery.

48. Glaisdale near Whitby at the height of its importance as an ironstone mining centre. It is dated 1872. Now little evidence of this era remains to be seen.

49. The lifeboat crew at Whitby taken before 1911. Even as long ago as this the National Lifeboat Institution was established.

50. Captain Cook's House. He is perhaps the most famous of all Whitby's sons and as a result of his exploits exploring the South Seas, the town of Whitby still maintains official links with places the other wide of the world including Tonga.

51. Barry's Yard, which is so typical of old Whitby, as it once was with tiered terraced cottages perching on the steep hill sides. This card, dated about 1910, was issued free with 'Shurey's Publication'.

Old Whitby, Boulby Bank.

52. The old cottages built in tiers on Bowlby Bank which have now been demolished. This card dates from about 1904 or 1905.

53. The original Wesley Chapel, opened by John Wesley himself on June 13th, 1788. It was originally approached through an alley with houses on either side, but R.E. Pannet bought the property and demolished it to open up the approach to the chapel.

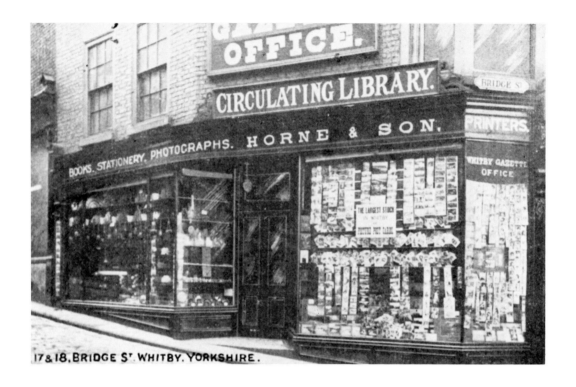

54. The Whitby Gazette Office in Bridge Street before 1918. In common with so many other stationers shops of this time they operated a circulating library before the advent of the public libraries. They also claimed the largest stocks of picture postcards in Whitby!

55. West Hill House, Whitby, one of many properties in Scarborough, Whitby and Hartlepools damaged by the shelling of the German navy on December 16th, 1914.

56. Wounded Belgian soldiers being nursed at Whitby during the First World War. Many large properties were converted to hospitals for the care of wounded soldiers during this period.

Ex-German Submarine U-98 in Whitby Harbour.—Length 247 feet.

57. The ex-German submarine U 98 on display in Whitby Harbour. It was 247 feet in length.

"Isle of Iona" ashore at Whitby, December 7th, 1906.

58. Many ships have come aground in or around the coast near Whitby. This is the Isle of Iona, aground at Whitby on December 7th, 1906. A crowd of folk are gathered by the lighthouse.

59. The Old Market Place, Whitby, as it looked in 1904. Much of this property has been pulled down in relatively recent years for road improvements. It is interesting to see that there was a commission agent Alfred Jefferson operating.

60. A fishing-boat with its tall masts just sailing out of the harbour making for the fishing grounds. Many of these boats were family owned going back two and three generations.

61. It is hard to imagine that a bridge of this size and construction at East Row Sandsend could be destroyed by floods.

WHITBY'S "WALKING MEN."

62. These two portable riggs were constructed for the building of the pier extensions at Whitby and were known locally as Whitby's 'Walking' men.

63. One of the portable riggs at Whitby about to go crashing into the sea. This happened on April 8th, 1912.

64. Flooding in the centre of Whitby during the 1930's outside the Station Hotel and Empire Theatre.

65. The lighthouse, known as The Highlights, at Whitby before 1907.

66. One of the typical old Whitby fishing families where the women baited the lines for their husbands. They are wearing the shawls, head scarfs and long aprons and have their children with them. As the card had an Edward VII stamp on, it is from between the period 1901 and 1910.

67. This two masted schooner, taken in Whitby harbour by the local photographer J.T. Ross, is the Margaret Nixon. The building on the right was Clarkson's Furnishing and General Warehouse.

68. The coastguard station and sands, complete with donkeys, as it was in 1905.

69. Fishermen's wives gutting herring with the Marine Hotel. Marsh Hill is in the background.

70. Ye Olde Ship Launch public house with Robert J. Breckon as licencee. The inscription says 'The Home of the Press Gang' where those who had consumed too much ale would be encouraged to join the forces. The board on the right reads 'Recruits Wanted for all branches of His Majesty's, Army apply to the recruiter or to any branch of the Post Office.' This card is dated 1915, during the First World War.

THE SANDS, WHITBY.

71. This card was published by T. Turner of Skipton. The writer had enjoyed the water carnival the previous evening, which was accompanied by a band and the Bohemian Choir. The bathing huts can be seen by the water's edge and bathing tents can be hired. All the ladies have long dresses or skirts to their ankles and the men are wearing straw boaters.

72. The packed Whitby West Cliff Promenade at the turn of the century with a coach and horses driving along it. It is obviously a scorching day as the ladies all have parasols up to protect them from the sun.

COTTAGE HOSPITAL.

73. The Women's Ward in the Whitby Cottage Hospital as it was in 1905. It was sent by a patient in the ward to Miss Bowron of Church Street, Whitby.

74. One of the local industries for which Whitby is famous is jet carving. This is a scene, undated, inside a jet carvers shop.

75. This card of Kettleness station on the old North Eastern Railway Line between
Whitby and Middlesbrough dates from the early part of this century and is by T. Watson
of Lythe, a prolific producer of postcards of the Whitby area in this period. The line
closed about 1958.

76. The Market Place in 1905 with many of the goods displayed on the floor and others in baskets or barrels. In the background is the Silver Grid Fish and Chip restaurant.